OPEN YOUR MOUTH

Jasmine Gray is a Northern writer and Writing Squad graduate. In 2021, she won the inaugural First Light Writer's Prize for her art criticism 'BARE' (Tilt, 2021). Since, she has been shortlisted for the Edge Hill MA Short Story Prize (2022) and long-listed for the Rebecca Swift Foundation's Women's Poetry Prize (2023). Her work has appeared in *Anthropocene, Carmen et Error, The London Magazine* and elsewhere. Her debut pamphlet, *Let's Photograph Girls Enjoying Life*, was published with Broken Sleep Books (2019).

Also by Jasmine Gray

Lets Photograph Girls Enjoying Life (Broken Sleep Books, 2019)

Open Your Mouth

Jasmine Gray

Broken Sleep Books

ISBN: 978-1-915760-31-9

Cover designed by Aaron Kent

Edited and typeset by Aaron Kent

Broken Sleep Books Ltd
Rhydwen
Talgarreg
Ceredigion
SA44 4HB

Broken Sleep Books Ltd
Fair View
St Georges Road
Cornwall
PL26 7YH

Contents

LIKE SMOKE

Amy Winehouse sits in a black leather chair and looks at me calmly. She holds mischief in her eyes, like she's daring me to do something fantastic. I trip over my words, slurring them, as they fight to be free of my mouth.

I tell her I once watched a recording of her performing in a small church in Ireland.

I tell her my three favourite songs:

> You know I'm no good
>
> What is it about men?
>
> Love is a losing game

I say I saw a tribute band perform *Frank,* in Belgrave Music Hall once. It was magical. The way I closed my eyes, the inside of my lids a promise of her presence. The way the crowd, dark shadows, moved like a freed cult, our bodies as one, pulsing black holes, the opening of a saxophone. The grit we felt between our teeth, crunching ivory, the smell of damp and metal in the air. The lights, how they flashed, strobing moments, vultures feasting. My body, its twists, the way the grooves of my hips turned to silk when I heard her voice. That moment, in a dream, about to fall not knowing what you will catch as you do.

She is calm for a moment, crossing and uncrossing her legs, flicking her black hair over her shoulder. A silence as deep as still water. She opens her mouth, just as I've started to speak again. Our words mangle together, bashful and awkward.

I think you saved my life /

I never performed in a church

Someone here is lying.

There's something
I can't quite shake –
a devilfish branding
in the dead night
I'm so frightened
of leaving
being something inherited

I cling to things that hurt me

Question myself again: what is it about men?

I've been digging around the inside of your chest when no one is looking

I've found things I don't understand

1. A black pencil
2. A silver egg cup
3. A scorched photograph

4. A lock of hair
5. An empty pocket
6. A dead bee

To avoid thinking
I replay the moment so often
You place the needle of a record player onto my palm
And out of my mouth fall all the things
I want to stay

I wasn't shocked because I had won

I was shocked because Tony Bennett

said my name

AND THE WINNER OF THE GRAMMY IS

In this world, where I only get what I want
I catch the moment like a soiled feather
Place it in pickle brine
Seal it in a snow globe

I want for her to only ever feel nice things
An octopod dictator:
I make Tony spend his life repeating her name

Repeat her name

Catch a feather

Seal it

a saintly caricature she enters through my ear canal a lukewarm whisper a pull and release of a current against a high street amongst flailing debris I feel her assess me from the inside out there's a ringing in my head like a fridge door left open flying insects thrashing against my eye lids inside sudden flashes I see the jaw of a monster he's saying her name over and over again this time as though three letters are formed of smoke spitting it out splattering acid scratch card headlines of crack and rock and stop and roll I feel her eyes inside my head falling back and back again breathless and wanting bones formed of stolen ivory I'm so scared of him entering I take whatever numbness is on offer a drip a needle or a fall into open space I realise all too late these hands around my throat the voice I had is almost lost I watch myself a strange ghost bumbling around the inside of a church the wires of an electric pole wrap around my ankle and drag me further an octopus uses its tentacles to resurrect me subject me once again there's a taste of rusting metal damp in the dark removing all my clothes the world a lost hum the end a snap inside something unhealable a tightrope against my bare feet a camera lets me see my bones are made of lead scratch away now how this feels a wart multiplying everything I know with this pain lodged exactly where it is

I'm left with no choice

HOW A FEMINIST KEEPS FALLING IN LOVE
WITH CATHOLICISM

In an attempt to imagine myself as a church,
I play organ music so loud the water of my ear canal curls in.

If this was not real, I would seal each entrance shut.

I keep reading blogs about women and god,
women and gods, women's gods, women gods,
god's women.

I keep seeing his face reflected back,
a kiss on the imprint of an iris,
stain on glass.

A master of no one, creator.
(He was accused of sexual assault last year)

When I blink, the gentle sway of letting in and blocking out light, the shadow of his face on stone, sun through a stained window. I wonder if he ever listens to organ music.

If this was not real life, I would seal the entrances shut.

I can't house what I can't remember –
the fragments haunt me.

I sat beside someone I loved, watched a brown leather world
unfold. Autumnal New York, bad acting.

There's something about men that always write themselves a
sidekick, a beautiful woman.

This is not real life.

October.

Some kind of distant organ playing,
a hooded figure, bells ringing.

I wonder if the women he writes himself fucking
know the echoes of the dark.

He thinks I'm a slaughterhouse.

A nice man.

Two people, late-night, walking home, New York, fall.

A pledge of sympathy or an advertisement – this could be real life.

Wound up in your arms, warmth is a double-faced comforter.
I remember his speech vividly. A spray of spit at the hard conso-
nants. Elongation of the final sound, silky the way some American
accents stretch.

Not cool man.

a New York night sways

travelling on the tide
and other women's stories
her key – a weapon -

happily after neat vodka
he walks slowly to not let
intimacy fade away.

a woman remains after the men
to mop the blood blisters
with the curl of her hair

he tries to call out
let her know he understands
he says louder and louder
                again

NOT   *COOL*   *MAN*

All these actors – all these lonely women –
we all know the echoes of the dark.

Our world is divided by a split-screen:
believers / non-believers
silence / slaughter

We take our seats and watch
together. The play of
women and gods and
women and gods and
women and gods –

SELECTED POEMS FOR CREEPS

decorative

your vulnerability is that you are a joke
you know you are a bruised peach
you can pinpoint the date and time it all began
you fear anyone who meets you now will know
you want to slip inside cool water
you will let him destroy you then wake up the next day
and do his dishes
you say okay and fine after saying no a thousand times
you realise this isn't what consensual means
you throw up
you think if you could bite into your bones they'd crunch like an
apple, not a nectarine
you want people to belong together
you belong to every man who has ever touched you
you realise love has an edge
you'll never have sex again
your thoughts will outlive you
you think souls exist but have nothing to do with morality
and everything to do with cool water
heaven is conditional
you decide to like people depending on whether they accept your
friend requests
you realise women are a metaphor and faking it
means you've never been loved
a shadow of it
maybe –

eating unsliced cucumber is an anarchist act

don't you think? I ask, slicing the pointed green tip
we're in a time of no sex but
half an hour before
we'd pressed against one another
all breath and hunger
you're barely listening
an artistic act? you repeat
can you cut me two slices?
tenderly, I slice two concentric slithers –
half-moons – promise myself:
this is not a metaphor
I know we're going to end but I don't know when
I think we're going to end or else
we'll continue in circles forever
the cucumber waits on the chopping board
in a pool of its own secretions
thinking death has surely met it
is it not tiring always thinking about cucumbers
and anarchism, like you're some kind of fucking
vegetable missionary? I want you to say
are you not exhausted, feasting on diluted pulp,
expecting fulfilment?
I want to pick up the cucumber and shove it so far down my throat
I choke
I wonder if you'd laugh or even look up
I wonder if it'd turn you on
who is looking at me while I look at this cucumber?
pathetic, parted from its head, pooled in its own wet
in a few years this will all make sense

in a few years there will be no proof this dead thing existed
for now, the cucumber waits
begging for disorder
I lift its willing body to my mouth
let my teeth grate a hole in the silence
I wonder what rot will find it first

I don't know how to tell you this

but I'm white cold like that too-late sensation of leaning over the draining board and realising all the knives are facing blade-up. I'm sweet and my mouth is filled with quicksand muscovado, tongue thumbing the graves of my empty gums. In the pit of my stomach lives an eclipsing sun. I step around the blind corner into oncoming traffic. I am the concrete smack of a papier-mache skull against the corner of a table-top. I am that moment at the cinema where you turn to your date and say ooooh. I felt that. I am a curling toe. The phantom hammer hitting your kneecap. As the blunt metal makes contact - I am a thousand standing court room ovations. I am the crunch of a snail's shell in the morning when you're outside bare foot. The avocado stone hitting the floor - green flesh splatter. I'm the moment at the threshold, knowing. I am the final warning, eviction-notice red font. I am the nail varnish chipping as the door scrapes over your foot. I am indulgent,

lick of salt on a throbbing wound.

Open Your Mouth

When I first realised my writing had adopted a new taste, I was visiting my mother in her new home. Her moving away had coincided with the global pandemic so we hadn't seen each other for some time. It was August and the summer was slowly sighing away.

We went on a walk, passing fields of wheat, corn, sunflowers, and then, an abattoir.

Screeches of pigs pierced the calm of the seaside air and hung like a heavy fog.

It was a sound that was hard to pin down – a dense pleading against unknown violence.

My chest felt suddenly tight, as though a blackout curtain I'd employed, to maintain unfamiliarity with their suffering, had been torn down.

My mum, lifelong vegetarian and animal lover, glanced briefly then looked on. Continuing to chat normally as we passed the scene.

Choosing ignorance.

Though unrelated, it reminded me of an experience I'd had at seventeen. After enjoying a night separately, my mother and I had planned to walk home together. I went to meet her in the pub local to my childhood home, the one she had now moved away from. As I entered, my mum's then-boss, unknown to me at the time, had spotted and was approaching me.

He was a middle-aged man with a love of hunting.

He didn't know who I was.

He approached quickly, planting both hands around my waist, blocking my path.

Forcing my body to face him.

I remember distinctly how wet his mouth was, drunk and spitting questions.

Well, what do we have here then?

My mum, again, looked on.

Choosing ignorance.

I've always been conscious of the way my body has been observed by men. Like a criminal behind one-way glass, I could feel my limbs bending out of order.

I watched men, watching me, watching myself become strange.

Looked at like a piece of meat.

Consumed.

As Carol J. Adams puts it: 'If animals are alive they cannot be meat. Thus, a dead body replaces the live animal'.

My limbs, then, adopted the strange haze of something dead.

I became a ghost.

As the pandemic continued to mutate and grow – so did my writing.

It had a focus on physicality. It was verb-heavy, each poem ritualistic, an instruction manual.

I realised – I was mirroring the language of cooking, the lexis of taste.

Spending so long being starved of pleasure, automatically, my body began to revolve around the small glimpses of joy available to it. I grew reaccustomed to cooking from scratch.

Skin hunger salvation was found through the kneading of bread; the salt-sweet tang of conversation through the seasoning of stock.

Taste became resistance.

The corresponding hunger became a pit for anger to prove.

Pleasure negated by need.

A full belly politicised by its very necessity.

There will never be the language available to discuss the horror in debating hunger. How can we forgive those who think we should go unfed?

Eating, and writing, becomes fuel for change

for compassion

for rage.

The more I used food as a vehicle to write through, the more I could not outrun this bitter taste.

The kitchen, a safe space, its history for holding women...

Carol J Adams' words trailing behind me, like smoke...

How much are we defined by what we put in our body?
What our tongues enjoy and endure?
How much we indulge in our tastes and how much we venture
outside of them?

I wish to be delighted by what enters my mouth and what
leaves it.

Chewing is a way to weigh the weight of a line.
A recipe, a goldmine for richness.
A poem as a meal – equal parts identity, culture, history.

Writing through food has offered me both softness and sensuality, a place for nourishment and self-pleasure. It has also helped serve my frustration, my anger, my pain. A carrier of history, a place to build something new.

Cooking and poetry are social choices we make – what we choose to share, and with what communities.

Who we uplift.

Who we make stronger.

Who turns away from ignorance,

and who prefers to drown in it.

Acknowledgements

Amy Winehouse, my first true love, is featured repeatedly in this pamphlet – namely the title 'Like Smoke' and its line 'Question myself again: what is it about men?'. The line 'I wasn't shocked because I had won, I was shocked because Tony Bennett said my name' is often credited to Amy following her 2008 Grammy win, though I couldn't find the source. I suspect it is misremembered.

The Carol J Adams quotation is taken from *The Sexual Politics of Meat* (Bloomsbury, 2015).

A huge thank you to *Anthropocene, The London Magazine* and the editors of *The Book of Bad Betties* (Bad Betty Press, 2021) where some of these poems first appeared.

Throughout 2022, I had poetry residencies with both The Poetry Business and New Writing North x The African Writer's Trust. Thanks to all three organisations for giving me space to write.

Thanks to The Writing Squad, as always, for being a constant source of joy, support and inspiration. I would not still be writing weird little poems without you. Thanks to Steve for keeping The Squad going.

Thanks to James Byrne & the other members of the fab four – Rachel, Paul and Vicky – for their invaluable support in the early stages of this work. Thanks to Aaron for taking a chance on me (again) and being a legend in the poetry community. BSB 4ever.

Charlie Baylis has been a great friend and an even better editor – this pamphlet would be rotting somewhere without his help in fleshing it out. P.S. I stole the chapter name 'Selected Poems for Creeps' from him.

Last but not least, thank you to my beautiful friends for their uncomplicated, unconditional love and for dealing with the rawest unloading of all the creep-based trauma: Ariana, Emma, Kayleigh and Keara, Bella, Harry, Amber and Liv, and my littlest friend, Ella.

LAY OUT YOUR UNREST